FUN FACT FILE: BUGS!

20 FUN FACTS ABOUT SPIDERS

By Therese Shea

Please visit our website, www.garethstevens.com. For a free color catalog of all our high-quality books, call toll free 1-800-542-2595 or fax 1-877-542-2596.

Library of Congress Cataloging-in-Publication Data

Shea, Therese
      20 fun facts about spiders / by Therese Shea.
   p.   cm. – (Fun fact file: bugs!)
Includes bibliographical references and index.
Summary: This book describes spiders, including their physical characteristics, habitats, and eating habits.
Contents: Wonderful world of spiders – Icky and awesome arachnids – Spider senses – Bizarre bodies – Webs and silk – Mom and dad spiders – Growing up spider – Smallest and biggest – Spider predators – Creepy but helpful!
ISBN 978-1-4339-8245-3 (hard bound)
ISBN 978-1-4339-8246-0 (pbk.)
ISBN 978-1-4339-8247-7 (6-pack)
1. Spiders—Juvenile literature   [1. Spiders]
I. Title 2013
595.4/4—dc23

First Edition

Published in 2013 by
Gareth Stevens Publishing
111 East 14th Street, Suite 349
New York, NY 10003

Copyright © 2013 Gareth Stevens Publishing

Designer: Sarah Liddell
Editor: Greg Roza

Photo credits: Cover, p. 1 Amy Johansson/Shutterstock.com; p. 5 (wolf spider) nico99/Shutterstock.com; p. 5 (garden spider) dmvphotos/Shutterstock.com; p. 6 Stefan Petru Andronache/Shutterstock.com; pp. 8, 11, 23 Cathy Keifer/Shutterstock.com; p. 9 Craig Taylor/Shutterstock.com; p. 10 Gary Ombler/Dorling Kindersley/Getty Images; pp. 12, 20 Visuals Unlimited, Inc./Robert Pickett/Visuals Unlimited/Getty Images; p. 13 Eugene Berman/Shutterstock.com; p. 14 Harry Rogers/Photo Researchers/Getty Images; p. 15 1983paco/Shutterstock.com; p. 16 Photo Researchers/Photo Researchers/Getty Images; pp. 18, 27 D. Kucharski & K. Kucharska/Shutterstock.com; p. 19 Mercieca Tony/Photo Researchers/Getty Images; p. 21 Ludmila Yilmaz/Shutterstock.com; p. 22 © iStockphoto.com/CathyKeifer; p. 24 iStockphoto/Thinkstock.com; p. 25 cyrrpit/Shutterstock.com; p. 26 sunsetman/Shutterstock.com; p. 29 (black widow) GK Hart/Vikki Hart/Stone/Getty Images; p. 29 (brown recluse) Larry Miller/Photo Researchers/Getty Images.

Printed in the United States of America

CPSIA compliance information: Batch #CW13GS: For further information contact Gareth Stevens, New York, New York at 1-800-542-2595.

Contents

Words in the glossary appear in **bold** type the first time they are used in the text.

Wonderful World of Spiders

You probably know something about spiders already. They're everywhere: city parks, country fields, and even your house! You know they have many legs and use webs to catch insects. You might even know that many spiders are **venomous**, though only a few could harm people.

There are about 42,000 **species** of spiders, and they all differ in some way. The more you read about spiders, the more you'll realize what amazing creatures they are. They'll seem a little less scary and a whole lot cooler!

Spiders are found on every continent except Antarctica. But they may have lived there in the past.

FACT 1

Spiders aren't insects.

Many people think spiders are insects, but spiders are

arachnids. While insects usually have wings, arachnids don't.

Their bodies are divided into two parts, while insects have three.

Arachnids have eight legs, not six. Arachnids also don't have

feelers, or antennae, as insects do.

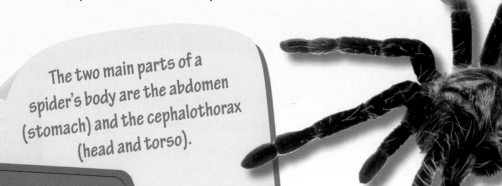

abdomen

cephalothorax

The two main parts of a spider's body are the abdomen (stomach) and the cephalothorax (head and torso).

Arachnids and Insects, Side by Side

arachnids	insects
two main body parts	three main body parts
no antennae	antennae
eight legs	six legs
no wings	wings (usually)

Spider Senses

FACT 2

Some spiders have no eyes.

Most spiders have eight eyes arranged in pairs on their head. But some have two, four, or six eyes. Others have none! These spiders live in dark places such as caves. Eyes wouldn't help them find food there.

About 99 percent of all spiders have eight eyes. Most of the rest have six eyes.

The arrangement of eyes on a spider's head depends on the species.

A spider's sense of sight depends on how they catch their food.

Hunting spiders—such as jumping spiders or wolf spiders—have excellent eyesight. They need it to spot **prey**. Web-building spiders often have poor eyesight. Luckily, they just need to feel prey moving in their webs to catch them. They may see changes in light, though.

FACT 4

Spiders can smell with their legs.

Spider legs aren't just for walking.
They're for sensing. Each leg is covered
with special hairs that can feel **vibrations**.
Movements of prey cause vibrations on
the ground and in a spider's web. Other
leg hairs actually sense smells in the air!

These are the legs of a Mexican red-kneed tarantula.

Bizarre Bodies

Spiders have two more legs that aren't really legs.

Pedipalps are attached to each side of a spider's mouth. They look like legs, but they're not. Pedipalps have special hairs that sense smells, too. Some spiders use them to hold prey. Parts of the pedipalps help some spiders crush food.

Some people mistake pedipalps for another pair of spider legs. But they work more like a pair of arms and a nose!

pedipalps

11

Spiders don't breathe through their mouth.

Some spiders have book lungs, which look somewhat like the pages of a book. As blood runs through the book lungs, it trades carbon dioxide for oxygen, just like we do when we breathe. Other spiders breathe through air tubes called tracheae (TRAY-kee-ee).

Air enters a spider's tracheae through tiny holes in its body called spiracles.

spiracle

FACT 7

Small spiders have really, really big brains.

Tiny web-spinning spiders have brains so big they spread into their legs! Scientists think a large brain helps a small spider spin its webs as well as large spiders do. The smaller the spider, the more space the brain takes up in the body.

Some spiders can walk on water.

Fishing spiders have long thin legs and light bodies—so light they can walk on water! When they need to hide from **predators**, they dive into water and stay there for over a half hour. Their book lungs get air from bubbles in the water.

Fishing spiders trap an air bubble with their legs when diving. This allows them to breathe underwater.

Crab spiders sit in places where they blend in with the surroundings. Their prey doesn't see them until it's too late.

chelicerae

All spiders have fangs.

Spiders grab prey with their chelicerae (kih-LIH-suh-ree). Each of these "jaws" ends in a **fang**. In most spiders, venom travels through the fang. It either **paralyzes** prey or turns its insides to liquid. Then the spider can drink its meal through its straw-like mouth.

Webs and Silk

FACT 10

Spiders make more than one kind of silk.

Most spiders have different silk **glands** for making different kinds of silk. For example, many female spiders make one kind of silk for weaving webs, another for wrapping eggs, and another for trapping prey.

Spiders spin silk using body parts on their abdomen called spinnerets. Most spiders have six spinnerets.

Spider Silk Types and Their Uses

silk types	uses
swathing	wrapping prey
web-making	catch prey
dragline	connect spider to web in case of fall
parachute/balloon	float in wind to find new food source
shelter	make tunnel or nest
egg sac	keep eggs safe
mating	males wrap cells to give to female when they **mate**

Not all spiders spin webs.

While about half of all spider species spin webs to catch their meals, the rest are hunters. Jumping spiders wait until prey is just a few inches away and then jump on it. However, they can jump more than 40 times the length of their own body!

jumping spider

FACT 12

Trap-door spiders like to play hide-and-seek with their prey.

Trap-door spiders dig a den in the ground and line it with silk. They make a door out of dirt and silk. When they feel a vibration above, they quickly swing open the door and give their prey a deadly bite.

Mom and Dad Spiders

FACT 13

Male spiders really show off for their mate.

When a male spider is ready to mate, he tries to interest a female. Hunting spiders "dance" by waving their legs or stomping on the ground. Jumping spiders show off colorful hairs. Web-building spiders pluck the female's web, almost like they're saying, "Look at me!"

Some male nursery-web spiders give females a gift before mating—a wrapped fly. If they can't find a fly, they just wrap a small stone!

This wolf spider mother carries her egg sac attached to her spinnerets.

FACT 14

Some female spiders lay 2,000 eggs.

Spider eggs look like a drop of water. While some mother spiders lay 100 or more eggs, others lay just one! They may put their eggs in one pouch, or sac, while some make several. They attach sacs to plants or carry them around.

Growing up Spider

Many baby spiders are born travelers.

Some young spiders stay near their mother. She helps them find food to eat. Others climb high, spin a long line of silk called a dragline, and let the wind carry them someplace else. This is called "ballooning."

Mother wolf spiders carry their babies on their back.

Young spiders can regrow a lost leg.

Young spiders shed their skin, or molt, as they get larger. They grow until they burst out of their old skin. This may happen up to 12 times before they're adults. If they lose a leg, they'll grow a new one when they molt!

Molting spiders aren't safe while their new outer skin, or exoskeleton, is drying. They can get hurt easily.

23

FACT 17

The smallest spider could stand on a pinhead.

Male spiders are usually smaller than the females of a species. Many people think the male *Patu digua* spider is the smallest spider in the world. The *Patu digua* measures just 3/200 inch (0.38 mm)! It can be found on the Southeast Asian island of Borneo.

This tiny jumping spider is resting on someone's hand.

The goliath tarantula makes hissing sounds, unlike most spiders.

FACT 18

The goliath birdeater tarantula would fill up a dinner plate.

The goliath birdeater tarantula may grow to be 1 foot (30.5 cm) across! It got its name because someone reported seeing one eat a bird. This tarantula's fangs can be 1 inch (2.5 cm) long. It lives in South American rainforests.

Spider Predators

Some spider predators just pretend to get caught in their webs.

Spiders do have predators, including lizards, snakes, frogs, and fish. One clever enemy—the **assassin** bug—pretends to get caught in a spider's web. When the spider feels its vibration, it runs over to bite it. Instead, the assassin bug kills the spider!

assassin bug

Spider wasps are the spider's worst enemies.

Spiders' nastiest enemy is the spider wasp. Spider wasps sting spiders, sometimes killing them and sometimes paralyzing them. Then they bring the spider to their young as a meal. Spider wasps will pick fights with much larger spiders.

This spider wasp has killed a wolf spider.

Creepy but Helpful!

Every species of spider is different—and only a very small number could actually hurt a person with their venom. In North America, this includes the black widow and the brown recluse. However, even these spiders would rather run away than bite.

One spider eats about 2,000 insects a year. These are insects that could otherwise be running around your house! Even more helpful are spiders that kill grasshoppers and other pests that eat the crops we depend on for food. So maybe spiders aren't so bad after all!

The black widow and the brown recluse are the most venomous spiders in North America. However, they rarely bite people.

brown recluse

black widow

Glossary

arachnid: one of a large class of small animals that includes spiders, scorpions, ticks, daddy longlegs, and mites

assassin: someone or something that kills with a sudden attack

fang: a long, pointed tooth

gland: a body part that produces something needed for a bodily function

mate: one of two animals that come together to produce babies. Also to come together to make babies.

paralyze: to make something lose the ability to move

predator: an animal that hunts other animals for food

prey: an animal that is hunted by other animals for food

species: a group of animals that are all of the same kind

venomous: able to produce a liquid called venom that is harmful to other animals

vibration: a rapid movement back and forth

For More Information

Books

Ganeri, Anita. *Tarantula*. Chicago, IL: Heinemann Library, 2011.

Lunis, Natalie. *Deadly Black Widows*. New York, NY: Bearport Publishing, 2009.

Morris, Ting. *Spider*. North Mankato, MN: Smart Apple Media, 2005.

Websites

How Spiders Work

science.howstuffworks.com/environmental/life/zoology/insects-arachnids/spider.htm
Learn more about spider parts and why they're some of the coolest animals on Earth.

Spider Sense: Fast Facts on Extreme Arachnids

news.nationalgeographic.com/news/2004/06/0623_040623_spiderfacts.html
Read some amazing spider facts—including what they taste like!

Index